Pauline Prior-Pitt

HOLDING CLOSE

SPIKE PRESS

HOLDING CLOSE

First published in 2010
by SPIKE PRESS, 112 Broomfield Road, Coventry CV5 6JZ

ISBN 1 872916 45 7

Set in Gar:
Printed an
by THOM
Kelvin Inc

Distributo
AVANTI
Arlington

All rights r
A CIP rec

Library

www.pauline-prior-pitt.com

ACKNOWLEDGEMENTS

I would like to thank the editors of the following publications
in which several of the poems first appeared: Riptide, New
Writing from the Highlands and Islands (*Two Ravens Press*),
Poetry Scotland, Markings, Artemis Poetry (*Second Light*),
Cleave, New Writing by Women in Scotland (*Two Ravens Press*).

'You' and 'Jewel' were commissioned by the Royal Aberdeen
Children's Hospital.

For Robert
with my love

THANKS

Grateful thanks as always to Sally McKeown, editor
of Spike Press, and to Daphne Powis for her acuity and
perceptive advice.
I would also like to thank Charlotte Pitt Miller, Jean Saffell,
Katharine Barr, and Betty Macaulay for their continued
support and encouragement during the writing.

CONTENTS

I

II

III

IV

I

BETWEEN

before dogs bark   between sleep and wake
words drift from my head to pen on paper

high winds frap my sheets
to tangled threads   and Isa and Donnie
wash their clothes in the loch   dry them on the fence

and the view is always the same
but never the same in the changing light
in this land of wind   and water   and stone

and sheep on the single track   refuse to move
and slow cows sway their pregnant bulk   on elegant legs
blank stare at me
                                and the short eared owl on its post
swoops off   low glides over the moor

it has to be like this   to pen on paper

no screen   no hum   no winking curser yet

1

ETERNITY

Even now in her mother's womb
as she floats in warm waters,
a foetus smaller than her mother's smile

even now, deep down,
she forms the tiny orbs
that will become her daughters.

MOTHER AND DAUGHTER

Shall we go
come with me
swim with me daughter
swim with me daughter
in the deep water.

Cold in the water
cold in the getting in
cold in the water.

Shall we go
come with me
swim with me daughter
into the folding waves
wallow in laughter.

Follow me, follow me
into the water
colder and warmer
warmer and colder
until we are floating.

Floating again
together in water
mother and daughter
in deepest water.

SOMEHOW LOST

He said she would have wanted me
to have them
his gift to her when I was born
but I was wearing Mary Quant
sacks in black above my knees
and wanted longer beads   much longer
to swing and twist in student bars
and left them in their box   for now

somehow   in all those moves   I lost

her soft pink beads threaded on gold
                in her lilac dress with matching coat
and small brimmed hat   never quite the right shoes

I missed her most when you were born
weaving our threads   her gift of beads

                                now your first child
and you consumed by mother love   and I for you
our early morning days glow red
overflow in holding close
catching up on sleep   and weeping

and this is when
I should be giving you the beads

instead you have a gift for me   they
are not quite the same   but almost
her soft pink beads threaded on gold

MOTHERS' DAY

Just inside the shop,
clutching a bunch of tired purple daisies,
a little girl, is sobbing, "But I wanted to give her
those roses."

And her father,
carrying too much Saturday shopping,
shoves her out of the door
muttering expense.

Those roses
are soft, pale, billowy pink,
and a woman buying half a dozen for herself
aches for the gift
of tired purple daisies.

SETTING OUT

On the slipway he shackles on white sails,
tightens her halyards, checks her engine,
slides her into the sea.

Wind on a lea shore and she refuses.
Over and over she ploughs back, curves
round to mount the slipway.

He wades in deep, heaves himself on board,
keeping her prow into the wind
until a lull allows him to propel her off shore.

Out in the bay her engine splutters -
like his cries those nights when he forgot to sleep
and I stood watching the moon hours rocking him-

splutters and fails.
Over and over he jerks the cord.
hanging on to the tiller to hold her into the wind.

Twice he hurls the anchor out
coiling rope, taking up the slack
looping it hand over hand until it holds.

And when it does,
I watch him hoist the mainsail and the jib.
See them stiffen in the wind.

VISITORS

Stay bright for them.

Don't overcast the sky
to disappear the hills
or settle thick mist
low down to the fence.

Don't show off
your veils of horizontal rain
or batter them with gale force winds.

Let them see

how sunlight turns
the headlands ochre, gold
and blushes distant hills,

how bays of sand
curve white
below the dunes,

how the sea is a fancy sapphire
far out, indigo,
and closer inland,
opal.

Let them see this.

But if dull grey
day after day
has to be your offering,

then gift one hour,
one moment only
of your dazzling bright,

for them to hold
when they go home.

ARRIVAL OF THE FERRY AT LOCHMADDY

It's still miles out in the Minch
but much closer than a dot on the horizon

and you won't see me   but I wave anyway

as you pass the Madadhs
a group on the outside deck looks like you
and I begin our wave
both arms in a sort of half star jump
without the jump   but jumping as well from time to time

and I'm not looking round
not caring who's looking at me   I'm focussed
focussed on the small group   but they don't wave back

then I catch my first sight
two big   two much smaller   higher up
than where I was looking   all doing our star jump wave

                                        at the end of the pier
I'm as close as I can get without falling into the sea
still waving   now yelling   and you're yelling back

berthing the boat takes   forever
before they hoist the steps up to the door
I'm waiting at the bottom

you are first off the boat

The Madadhs are two rocks at the entrance to Lochmaddy bay

STUFF

They don't like it
when their old bedroom
becomes the spare room

when you ask them to remove their stuff
and they say
what stuff
and you say
that stuff in the chest of drawers
stuff in the wardrobe
stuff in boxes under the bed

and they say
oh that stuff
there isn't room in my flat for that stuff

and you say
it has to go
and will they come and sort it
take what they want and you'll get rid of the rest
and they say
yes they'll come

and they come
but they don't sort it or take it
and it stays

and you offer to sort it for them
but they say
no they'll sort it
and it stays

until the day comes when
you empty the stuff in the drawers
and the wardrobe
into black plastic sacks
and put them in the hall
by the front door
with the boxes from under the bed
ready for them to collect
but they don't collect

and you move the sacks and boxes into the garage
out of the house
and it's a squeeze to park the car
but they're out of the house

And by the time they come and take them away
if ever they do
other boxes are under the spare bed
boxes of toys
for their children to play with
when they come to stay.

MEN COMPLAIN

How women say
they don't want a sandwich
but when you've nearly finished yours
always ask for a bite.

How when you ask them
if they'd like a piece of toast
always ask for half a slice.

How in restaurants
they always want a taste of what you're having,
leaning over the table to fork up a mouthful
which isn't polite.

Then they want to share a pudding.

It's a food thing.

DO IT YOURSELF

Look, I said, this time you need a plan.
You could start by dividing the light from the dark.
and you could call the lightness, day.
and the darkness, night.
He showed no interest at all, not a spark.
I filled up his glass.

You could build a firmament
and divide the waters under the firmament
from the waters above the firmament.
You could call the firmament, heaven.
He could see what I meant
but he wasn't impressed.

And what if you were to gather
all the waters under heaven into one place
until dry land appears.
You could call the dry land, earth
and the gathered waters, sea.
And the earth could bring forth grass,
herb yielding seeds, fruit yielding trees.
He couldn't agree.

And in the heavens,
if you had time, and you wanted to,
you could fix up some lights
create seasons, days, months, years
hang two chandeliers;
the greater one to shine by day
the lesser one by night.

And in the waters,
you could fashion many creatures that have life,
luminous fish in the waters;
not all luminous of course.
And birds, birds to fly above the earth
in the open firmament of heaven.
And, this is just a suggestion, but you could bless them
tell them all to be fruitful and multiply.
I felt a slight interest at last
and refilled his glass.

And on the earth
you could bring forth living creatures after their own kind,
and cattle, cattle, and creeping things
and beasts of the field.

And that was when he leant towards me and said,
"And man. Yes! I will make man.
He shall be in my own image, after my own likeness.
And he shall have dominion.
He shall have dominion over the fish of the sea,
and the fowl of the air, over the cattle, and over all the earth,
and over every creeping thing that creepeth."

And I shouted, "No! No! No!
Not man, not man in your own image
to have dominion over the whole earth,
over fish and fowl, over cattle,
and over every creeping thing that creepeth.
Not man. Not dominion.
That is not what I had in my plan."

14

He left before I finished speaking,
strode out muttering something about sheds.

If only I had been more diplomatic
if I hadn't been so adamant... about man.
I should have laid back, persuaded him to wait,
but it was too late.

There was an almighty bang.
And all at once,
the darkness was divided from the light.

CRUMBS

It would seem that men
have a different relationship to crumbs.
They like to see them on the breadboard
with a fair scattering across the surfaces.

They seem to need crumbs to be there.
Even when you clear them away,
clean every one off the board,
wipe every surface before you leave,

on your return, they will be there.
Crumbs all over again
with maybe even a buttery knife
and a jar of marmite with its lid off.

You wonder if this is supposed to be a piece of art.
an installation based on still life:
"crumbs scattered on board
with unlidded marmite and buttery knife".

Maybe you are frustrating his artistic talent
constantly wiping away his attempts.
This could be a work in progress to be left day after day,
for weeks, months even, until it is complete,

when it can be moved, on a day without wind,
into the Gallery of Modern Art,
displayed with his artist's statement
about waste, poverty and frustration.

Who knows what might happen.
If he was feeling hungry at the time
and fancied, a simple meal of bread, butter and marmite
maybe Saatchi or someone will buy it.

But of course, men don't say.
And until they do
you carry on
wiping all their crumbs away.

INSTALLATIONS FOR THE GALLERY OF MODERN ART

The artist has declined to offer a statement to accompany these domestic pieces except to state that there is no significance in their order. They could be seen as simultaneous.

wet towels
in heaps
on tiled floor

jeans   T shirts   pizza   socks
duvet   towel   Green and Blacks
mugs   trainers   bottles   cans
pants   biscuits   books   ash
no sign of bedroom carpet

fridge
with
door open
for no
apparent reason

Guardians
and Heralds
piled on stool
some
fallen
o
f
f

lights on
in bedroom
bathroom
landing
hall
living room
kitchen
no one in

beer glass
balanced on
vest
resting on
radio
on cluttered table
beside bed
with sleeper unknown

empty
weetabixy bowls
empty
mugs with floating mould
poked under sofa

II

LABYRINTH WOMEN

They scrape the labyrinth into soft sand with sharp sticks,
use long string for measuring,
carry a rock to be the centre stone.
And then the blessing, there has to be a blessing.

They wait for someone to walk in.
One washes her feet in the sea,
searches in the water for a pebble,
chooses smooth quartz.

And now they're walking in, walking to the centre,
now walking towards, now walking away,
now with sun on their faces, now in shadow,
making shallow footprints, always getting closer.

Some women are ahead, still walking in,
others are already walking out,
all on the same path.
As they pass they hold each other for a moment.

Women at the centre sit still,
eyes closed, hands open in their laps.
Before they leave they stoop to place their pebbles
on the centre stone, with all the others.

And women walk ahead, still walking out.
Others walk towards, still walking in.
As they pass they hold each other close…

SEPIA WOMAN
studio photograph of an unknown relative

Did someone tighten the bun
in the nape of your neck and scrape back
your hair from its straight centre parting?

Not a wisp slips out of place,
to dance on your forehead or tickle thin eyebrows
above such solemn bright eyes.

You have given my sister your firm square chin
and are blamed for the fleshy tip of my nose.
No other clues, except for your collar.

We would choose this satin and lace
sewn on top of a crochet collar,
spreading out to the seam of our sleeves,

this frivolous bow, silk bow on silk bow,
ten ribbon ends showing.
                    So, why the straight face?

Is someone making you sit very still?
We press our lips together like this
to stop ourselves from giggling.

BLUE GIRL
for Jean

She's a blue   girl.
An eyes of blue   girl.
An almost any shade
of blue will do   girl.

Whatever she buys   it has to be   blue.
Whatever she wears   it has to be   blue.

Red   and blue.
Pink   and blue.
Hardly ever green   and blue.
Lots and lots of   navy blue.

It suits her through and through.
She's a true   blue   girl.
True to me and you   blue girl.

And when she wears it   she looks stunning in black!

CONCERT

These two girls have edge.
They like to do it standing up.

One, older than she looks, spikes her cello on a chair,
resting its neck on her bared shoulder,
her head thrown back, smiling.

Clarsach plays side on, her long dark hair a curtain
as she leans in close, spinning silk
from taut strings dancing waterfalls.

Now Cello plays her bow wide across the strings
and long low notes vibrate our very bones
as she begins to sing old Scottish songs.

And in this ancient hall with arrow slits,
we sit like peasants, let inside to feast on music
played for Lairds and Kings,

who, when the music's done, might take
these standing girls and lie them down.

NOTHING TO SAY

They should have taught me how to speak to my Grandmother.
The memory of chocolate cake soggy with treacle
and the back kitchen smelling of gas, is not enough.

At the time of the treadle sewing machine,
where I clattered for hours with the leather loop off
while they sat face to face on the horse-hair sofa,

mouthing their words in slow motion, spelling
quickly with fingers, telling me there would be cake
and grandma liked my pinafore dress.

They should have cut back the laurel over the windows.
It was as if she had something to hide
from people who thought she was mad,

who laughed at her crab fingers signing,
at her mouth broken apart in exaggeration,
rasping words they couldn't understand.

They should have shown me how to make my fingers
join in their pantomime, grandma the witch.
"Touch Grandma's arm if you want to speak to her", they said.

But then I had nothing to say.

SHE HAD NO UMBRELLA
poetry workshop exercise

"She had no umbrella".
As she wrote these words
her pen ran out
and she reached for another...

"She had no umbrella"
if she walked in the rain
she would only get wet
what did it matter...

"She had no umbrella"
no father or mother
no sister or brother
no lover...

"She had no umbrella"
Her dress was thin
she got soaked to the skin...

This isn't the way to write a poem
about "she, no umbrella
and maybe rain". Start again!

So, this girl without an umbrella,
couldn't she buy one
as soon as she got into town?
But if it rained she'd be soaked by then.

It might not rain.
Is rain implicit in the line
"she had no umbrella"?

It could be just a thought.
As you watch a darkening sky
or a cloud passes over the sun,
you do think "no umbrella".

You do, it can ruin your day,
unless you are one of those people
who always wear coats with hoods
or who say "well it's only water".

But what if she's wearing a summer dress,
meeting someone special
on a first date
and she's done her hair
and makeup and everything,

and her mascara runs like liquorice
down her face and she doesn't know,
and he sees her looking like that,
like a soaked little waif.

This makes him feel strong and protective of course,
and he just adores her,
carries her off to his hotel room
where she can soak in hot bubbles
look cute in his towelling gown.

He orders champagne and she giggles
and somewhere in the distance
an orchestra plays
and he tells her he loves her
asks her to marry
and the towelling gown
falls from her shoulders
and they end up in bed.

Well they would,
they would if this was a film.

But it's not,
it's a poem.

She had no umbrella
and it didn't rain.

DAD'S PIPE

How he always sat in the pink chair,
chewing on it, pointing with it
to make a point.

How his short nails gripped the blade
of his pen knife, levering it open
to scrape out the bowl.

How he leaned into the fire place
knocking it on the tiles
to shake out the ash.

How he patted his pockets finding his pouch,
dividing the flat tobacco into fine strands,
poking it into the bowl, tamping it down.

How he struck the match towards him,
holding it over the tobacco, sucking on the stem,
then leaning back, exhaling grey smoke.

How mother always hated the foul smell
filling the living room; the taste
on her lips when he kissed her.

VISITING HENRY MOORE'S
DRAPED RECLINING FIGURE

So perfectly captured in bronze,
one can't resist stroking,
though we're not supposed to.

She's out of proportion of course, all his women are.
Such a small head on her slender neck,
breasts like egg cups.

And then her whole weight
the weight of her
sunk to her belly, her bottom, her dough heavy thighs.

Is she ready to give birth in this reclining pose?
Love the drapery suggesting a dress.
Wonder why he left her breasts exposed?

HENRY MOORE'S
DRAPED RECLINING FIGURE

Keep stroking. Warm my frozen bronze
with your woollen gloves. Even children
sitting astride would be welcome at this moment.

Fancy him leaving my breasts exposed
in this flimsy verdigris dress.
What was he thinking of?

And sculpting me like an avocado.
It's not my fault. He carved his women big.
He chose to chisel thunder thighs.

And I don't think
he cast my head so small, to indicate,
'small brain just fit for motherhood'.

And no I'm not about to drop a baby.
Look between my legs, everyone does.
There's nothing there.

Of course he wouldn't know I'd end up cold,
outside in Yorkshire. I should have been displayed
indoors, or outside somewhere warmer.

If only I could shift from off this plinth
I'd cosy to the gardener's bonfire. It can't be far away.
I can smell the smoke from here.

MUCH MORE THAN NAMES
for the Three Islands International Artists Workshop on North Uist

Our names are strangers
in each others mouths.
We shape the sounds.

Names fizz like sherbet on the tips
of foreign tongues, as we try
to remember them.

Each day we work together or apart,
make tangible our thoughts
about this place, respond,

rearrange old stones, slice peat,
tie ribbons on to posts, fashion
our environmental art

to leave a presence here
something of ourselves
when we depart.

And when we leave with promises
to meet again, names slip
between our lips, easy as our own.

We take, and leave behind
much more than names
when we go home.

MEETING AT THE MOBILE LIBRARY VAN

In your muddy coat, you stroll up from your croft;
choose two biographies.

And I'm not sure you'll want
to look at poetry; am surprised

when the pirate behind your fiery eyes
lets me help you choose a Douglas Dunn
to add to your collection.

Quick as a dog you're down at the loch side
showing me your veg patch,
hidden from storms inside peat stacked walls.

"Bloody deer have eaten all my greens."

You ask if I like beetroot, tug up
two huge globes covered in mud.
Each one must weigh at least a pound.

And I've been waiting for this windy day
to open windows wide,

chopping the beets with onions and Bramleys
adding sugar, spice, and vinegar
and slowly simmering them together.

And I'm thinking, six jars of chutney
are more than a fair exchange

for the poetry we chose for you to relish.

ROUTINE

All the chairs?
Yes all the chairs.

All the chairs piled on top of the tables?
Yes all the chairs piled on top of the tables.

All the chairs in every room?
All the chairs in every room, for the cleaner.

For the cleaner of course.
All the chairs piled on top of the tables for the cleaner.

All the chairs piled on top of the tables
for the cleaner we never saw,
for the cleaner who came after we left.

Who swept the dust
lifted bits of cut paper
picked up sharpened shavings.

Who mopped the floor bereft of chairs
left it in that wet state
left it for a while to dry

and mopped more floors in corridors
more rooms with chairs all piled on top of tables
more and more mopped floors…

Then all the chairs lifted down

All the chairs?
*Yes all the chairs lifted down and placed four square
at every table.*

All the chairs placed four square at every table
in every room?
In every room.

And then go home?
And then go home.

And the next day?
The same again.

THE CHOSEN

With my back to the sea
a whole beach of pebbles
heaped in huge waves
between me and the sky

and like a god I stoop to choose
small flat oval shapes
blacker than liquorice cakes
to add to my collection.

Others might choose
orbs of opaque quartz
or speckled pebble eggs.
I have been tempted.

But from this congregation
my pebble universe
these small flat ovals
are the chosen shapes,

each one arranged
within the rest of my selection
settled on my heaven shelf.
It could be their idea of hell.

DOODLING

She's doodling
in the margins
filling her edges
with wild flowers
drifting weeds.

She should be drawing rocks.

THRESHOLDS

Poised on thresholds
forgetting what she's come to fetch,

retracing her steps
until she can remember

is commonplace and she accepts.

Opening doors, hoping to find flour
in the cupboard
where she's always kept bowls,

looking for folded towels
in the drawer
where she keeps knives and forks,

opening the dishwasher
holding milk for the fridge,

is not what she expects.

WORDS

She can't remember the word,
stands open mouthed
waiting for it to arrive,
can't even think of a substitute.

Hours later it pops up
out of the blue,
too late to use.

NAMES

You know her name...
famous actress...
name begins with... 'L'
she was in...
that film called...
you know the one...
with that other actress...
what's-her-name...from Liverpool...she's in everything...
and that old actress from the television series...
what's it called... you know...
the one with two old tortoises mating at the beginning...
and that motherly actress in Larkfording Candle Rise ...
she played the piano for the WI..

And they all took their clothes off...

Do you mean 'Calendar Girls'?
That's it, Calendar girls.

With Julie Walters?
No not her, the other one.

Helen Mirren?
That's her, Helen Mirren.

You said her name began with 'L'.
Well I knew there was an 'L' in there somewhere.

TRAPPED

Like birds trapped
inside her head

their wings
tangled

in the net
of her brain

fluttering
in her tight throat

filling her mouth
with feathers;

sounds
struggle to escape

when making
the smallest word

is too much
to ask.

POEM

On waking they lie
side by side
eyes still closed.

He wonders aloud
what they will eat
for lunch.

He tells her
how he plans
to spend the day.

She plans a poem,
which begins,
'on waking
they lie side by side
in silence'.

SQUARING

She wants to restore the ruined byre
to how it was, old dry stone walls

four square facing out to sea
a summer shelter from south westerlies.

He wants to extend the shape
into a semi circle, making it look different.

And it is this difference lumps her throat;

how he must always be different
when sameness can restore a symmetry,

how crofts and sheilings here all stand
square on to states of gales and storms,

how often half circles are his answer
when hers would favour squares.

A STEADY CLIMB

After days of panic wind and rain
an early morning stillness when we wake,
an unexpected offering of calm.

Although I would prefer to walk beside
the sea, today we choose the forest walk;
a steady climb between the pines, along
the path that streams with last night's heavy rain.

We walk in silence, holding off our words,
letting early bird song charm our ears
and occupy our minds, until we speak
those thoughts, not easy now between us;

our long held promises of sicknesses
and health, holding close to what is left
to both of us of forests and of seas.

PERFECT ENOUGH
for Robert

Choosing this jug together from the potter's reject box,
we love its tall, slim shape, the wavy top
curving to the lip, its deep brown glaze, the way

it isn't perfect,
but perfect enough sharing white walls
with a blue sofa and an orange chair.

In other houses where we live
green glass shapes, candlesticks, and wooden bowls
take pride of place against dark patterned walls

and our less perfect jug
stands on shelves in other dusty rooms
for over forty years, until

as if by chance, we find another in an artist's shop,
not quite as tall and slim, smaller, with a paler glaze,
its wavy top still curving to the lip.

In our new room, against white walls,
we love the way
the two jugs hold together in a symmetry.

TRAVEL

Saturday morning she reads
the Guardian travel section;
files St Petersburg away
in *city breaks,* until some day when she flies off.

She knows some cities off by heart
places to see, places to stay, places
not to visit after dark.

Budapest and Bucharest are there
and Prague; she should see Prague.
Not Naples; she's not ready yet for Naples
but she knows it's in her file.

GRANDSONS

Grandsons catch
glimpses of elders
in a turn
a look
a lifted head
a way of walking out of doors
a laugh
a gentleness
a steady gaze
from eyes
that make you feel the child again
a levelling.

WHEN I AM OLD

When I am old take me out
to stand at the edge of the sea,

spray from the waves-break
on my face, salt wind licking my skin,

and the long stare out to the wide dark line
where the sea drinks down the sky.

IV

SEPARATE

like pebbles
randomly cast on shore
by the indifferent sea

near to each other
far apart   overlapping
crunched together

each holding separate   alone
in sun   in shadow

A VERY SERIOUS POEM ABOUT DEATH

Early morning in my nightie
attempting to write
a very serious poem about death

but leave off
to wash and dress
eat breakfast

and bins under the sink
one for organic
stinking of fish skins

the other for plastic
must be taken out
to the bin by the gate

and people phone
needing to know the theme
for the poetry evening

and out of date fruit
apricots, figs and prunes
demand to be stewed

and a card to send
to a friend in hospital
must be posted today

and a very serious poem about death
still at the brainstorming stage
waits on the page.

DEATH

She clings to my lips, my breath,
covers my breasts when I dress,
strings pearls round my neck
fashions her words in my mouth.
"Forever," she says. And again,
"Forever," and "Never, ever, again."

And in bed, her head on the pillow
with mine, the nightmare screams,
dreams caught in her cloak,
falling into the depths below.

And day after day at the sea, she
beckons me in to the slow dancing waves,
splashes my face, licks my cold skin,
swims below me, above me, beside me,
twists her legs round me,
pulls me close in to kiss,

whispers the bit about less
than a grain of sand in the surf,
and never again, and forever.
She knows about this.

SO

So, it will just be like
a dreamless sleep of nothingness
from which I never wake.

I will not know.

Is that supposed to comfort me
to never wake again?

In my waking hours,
I long for the deep forgetfulness
of sleep each night,

from which I wake
at first light,
to the dread threat

of the long sleep of nothingness,
from which I know
I never wake.

CANNOT

You cannot comfort me;

tell me I will not
slip into that long sleep
from which I never wake;

tell me I will not
decay, my ears and eyes stopped,
returned to gaping earth,

or burned to ash and scattered on the wind.

You cannot comfort me;
tell me I will not.

SHALL I ?

shall I die first
to save myself
the pain
of losing you

and leave you
grieving
on your own

or shall I let you go
and bear alone
the pain
of losing you

we both must wait
it is not ours
to choose

THE DEAD

They walk with you
the dead.

Some skip along in front
some walk beside
some, like naughty children,
drag behind.

Others walk on top of you
crush you into nothing
or demand to be carried
like shopping.

A few slip like loose change
into pockets.

And one or two
lie curled together,
stitched into the lining of your heart.

SHADOW

I would become a shadow
black on black, grey on grey
fading out of the light

to see you all grow tall
like weeds in the grass
warming your faces in the sun,

and like rosebay willow herb
making a party out of a wasteland.

I would become a shadow to see this.

YOU

you are my grief
you are my disbelief

my darkness and my light

you are bright sunshine
and the weeping rain

you are the sleeping leaves
the splash of waves

you are the vanished garden
the silent swing

you are the flight of birds
the sharp remembering

you are my everything

and when I light this candle
and say your name

you are the candle
you are the flame

Commissioned by the Royal Aberdeen Children's Hospital
for the annual service for bereaved parents and their families

JEWEL

Oh spring
you have snatched away
my jewel

cast away
sun diamonds
from my summer days

cut off
ripe rubies
from my autumn trees

Oh spring
you have led me
straight to winter jet

Commissioned by the Royal Aberdeen Children's Hospital
for the annual service for bereaved parents and their families

NIGHT WAVES

Wind batters my car
from side to side on the single track.
Rain smacks the windscreen.
The only light, my main beam
reflects the passing place up ahead.

On Radio 3, Paul Muldoon
lilts his new book, Horse Latitudes,
where the wind is light, days hot and dry.
Iraq, war, a musical instrument made from a horse,
skull, skin and hair, the death of his sister.

Unthinkable, a sister, death,
in the same breath
but I think it.
Grip the wheel to steady the car.
No light and the battering wind.

GRIEF

She is winter now.
Her gaze shrunk to a window pane.

Grass torn from tussocks
scatters to the fence.

Veils cover distant hills.
Sea and sky dissolve into the same grey.

Wild geese, in loose formation,
cry, " gone, gone, gone."

DEEP

From rock pools, wet, delicious
I kept your precious pebbles

held them wet in my mouth
like jewels, slipped them

our secrets, under my skin.

Now they are dull, dry,
and weighting the secret places

clustered too deep
to set down on the shore
for you to see.

FUNERAL

Gathered here together once again
to say farewell to another friend,
more funerals now than weddings.

To celebrate the life, not mourn the dead
not as easily done, as said.

She's gone, and maybe I'll be next
I'm one of the dying generation.
But not yet, please, not yet

I still haven't been to Marrakech,
never found that perfect dress,
not caught up with old dear friends.

So much to do before life ends.

And after life, what then? What then?

NOT IN PERSON

It will be a marvellous party,
one where everyone comes;
the family of course, that's expected,
and all my close friends will be there,

but this is a party
where cousins and relatives not seen for years
will drive for miles in motorway traffic,

where people abroad will travel on camels,
cross the desert to catch a plane,
(well that would be nice but it's highly unlikely)

where colleagues, acquaintances,
even people I hardly know,
will all make the effort to come.

Dave Brubeck will play (not in person of course)
"Take Five" makes a party swing.
Champagne and smoked salmon as people arrive.
lots and lots of champagne.

No tables to sit at, people will mingle,
mingling's much more fun.
And waiters will hover
and serve delicious finger food.

They'll talk about me of course they will,
they all have their memories.
And they'll say what a shame I can't be there.

People always say that.
"What a shame she can't be here.
She would have loved it all."

So I'm planning a marvellous party now.
But will people make so much effort to come
if it's not for my funeral?